UNCOVERING HISTORY
ANCIENT ROME

First published in 2001 by McRae Books
Copyright © 2001 McRae Books Srl,
Florence (Italy)

Everyday Life in Ancient Rome
was created and produced by McRae Books
Borgo Santa Croce, 8 – Florence (Italy)
e-mail: mcrae@tin.it

SERIES EDITOR Anne McRae
TEXT Neil Grant
ILLUSTRATIONS Manuela Cappon, Lorenzo
Cecchi, Matteo Chesi, Ferruccio Cucchiarini,
Luisa Della Porta, Sauro Giampaia,
Sabrina Marconi, Paola Ravaglia, Andrea
Ricciardi di Gaudesi, Giacomo Soriani, Studio
Stalio (Alessandro Cantucci,
Fabiano Fabbrucci, Andrea Morandi)

GRAPHIC DESIGN Marco Nardi
LAYOUT Laura Ottina, Adriano Nardi
EDITING Susan Kelly and Anne McRae
REPRO Litocolor, Florence
PICTURE RESEARCH Susan Kelly

Published in the United States by Smart Apple Media
1980 Lookout Drive, North Mankato, Minnesota 56003

Printed and bound in Italy

Library of Congress Cataloging-in-Publication Data
Grant, Neil, 1938–
Everyday life in ancient Rome / by Neil Grant ; [illustrations by Manuela
Cappon ... et al.].
p. cm. — (Uncovering history)
Includes index.
ISBN 1-58340-249-7
1. Rome—Social life and customs—Juvenile literature. I. Title: Ancient
Rome.
II. Cappon, Manuela. III. Title. IV. Series.

DG78.G73 2003
937—dc21   2002036613

First Edition
9 8 7 6 5 4 3 2 1

UNCOVERING HISTORY

Neil Grant

ANCIENT
EVERYDAY LIFE IN
ROME

Illustrations by Manuela Cappon, Luisa Della Porta,
Paola Ravaglia, Andrea Ricciardi di Gaudesi, Studio Stalio

Smart Apple Media

Table of Contents

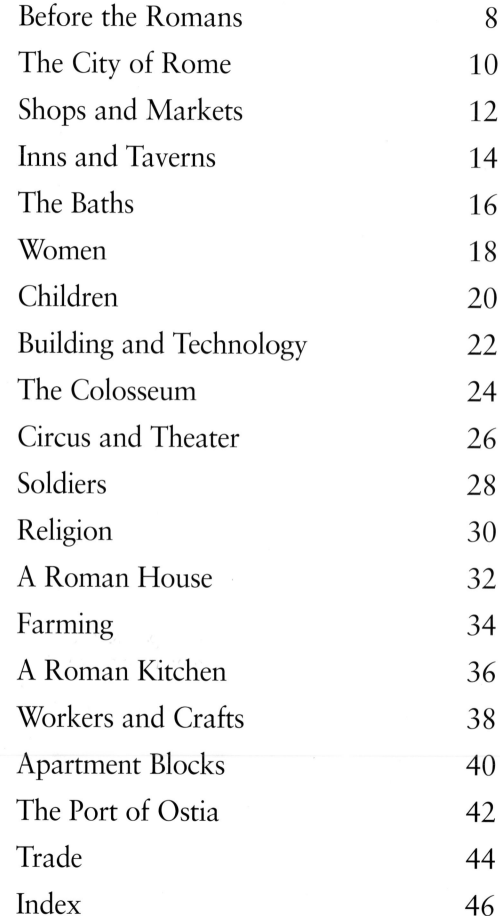

Before the Romans	8
The City of Rome	10
Shops and Markets	12
Inns and Taverns	14
The Baths	16
Women	18
Children	20
Building and Technology	22
The Colosseum	24
Circus and Theater	26
Soldiers	28
Religion	30
A Roman House	32
Farming	34
A Roman Kitchen	36
Workers and Crafts	38
Apartment Blocks	40
The Port of Ostia	42
Trade	44
Index	46

Introduction

In 700 B.C., Rome was no more than a few peasants' huts, but it grew to become the center of a great empire. About 500 B.C., the Romans threw off Etruscan rule and established a republic. By 300 B.C., the Roman Republic dominated Italy, and by 200 B.C., it had destroyed its chief rival in the Mediterranean, Carthage. But while its territory expanded, the Republic was in trouble, with civil war, dictatorship, and rivalry between army leaders. Julius Caesar seized power in 46 B.C. but was assassinated by men who feared he would make himself a monarch. That actually happened under his heir, who became the first Roman emperor, Augustus. Some early emperors were bad rulers, yet the Empire continued to grow. From the late first to third century A.D., the "Roman peace" brought general prosperity to an empire that, by 117, stretched from Scotland to Syria, including northern Africa. But by about 150, the Empire was on the defensive against envious neighbors. From the third century it began a long decline, until it was finally overthrown in 476.

For 1,000 years after the fall of the Empire, Roman civilization remained the model for Europeans. The Roman language, Latin, was the common language of educated people until the 16th century. Roman law is the basis of much modern European law even now. The Roman Empire was an international civilization. It included people of many religions and languages who were united under Roman government. The title "Holy (meaning Christian) Roman Emperor" was held by the leading European ruler until 1806. It could even be argued that the European Union is another attempt to regain the unity that the Romans first achieved.

Chronology of Ancient Rome

BEGINNINGS OF ETRUSCAN CIVILIZATION
about 800 B.C.

FOUNDATION OF ROME
753 B.C.

FOUNDATION OF ROMAN REPUBLIC
509 B.C.

ETRUSCAN CIVILIZATION DECLINES
from about 400 B.C.

FIRST PUNIC WAR
264 B.C.–241 B.C.

SECOND PUNIC WAR
218 B.C.–204 B.C.

THIRD PUNIC WAR
149–146 B.C.

CONQUEST OF GAUL
58–51 B.C.

BEGINNING OF IMPERIAL RULE
27 B.C.

CONQUEST OF BRITAIN
A.D. 43

ROMAN EMPIRE AT ITS GREATEST EXTENT
A.D. 116

EMPIRE DIVIDED INTO EAST AND WEST
A.D. 286

VISIGOTHS SACK ROME
A.D. 410

VANDALS CAPTURE CARTHAGE
A.D. 439

VANDALS SACK ROME
A.D. 455

FALL OF THE ROMAN EMPIRE
A.D. 476

Before the Romans

Nearly 3,000 years ago the people of Iron-Age Italy belonged to a large number of different tribes. Living in tribal villages, they were farmers and hunters and, by about the eighth century B.C., skillful craftspeople, too. Around that time, a new, more advanced culture developed in Etruria (Tuscany). These Etruscan people formed many small city-states, which often fought against each other. Rome was ruled by Etruscan kings until 509 B.C., when the last king was driven out and a republic was founded.

We know very little of the early people of Italy, except through objects, such as this metal incense burner, that archeologists have found in their graves.

These little figures were made in Sicily nearly 3,000 years ago. They probably represent a man and his wife, perhaps the occupants of the grave where they were found.

An Iron-Age village

The village that became Rome on the Palatine Hill (where the vast palaces of the Roman emperors would one day stand) may have looked like this 3,000 years ago. The people raised crops and animals, and they seem to have been fond of horses, as many bits of harness have been found in their graves. Their huts had walls of mud on a frame of sticks, with thatched roofs. The hill site gave some security against attack.

This small bronze figure of a caped warrior carrying a sword and staff (left) may be a tribal god or hero. Figures such as this were made by the people of Iron-Age Sardinia.

Etruscans and Greeks

The Etruscans were the most advanced people in Italy before the rise of Rome. They influenced the Romans, and were themselves influenced by the Greeks, who had established colonies in southern Italy. Between 500 and 200 B.C., the Romans conquered most of Italy, including Etruria and the Greek colonies.

This head of a goddess (right) was made in Rome by an Etruscan craftsman who had been influenced by Greek art. The mysterious smile was a trademark of early Greek and Etruscan sculptors.

This warrior (right) wears an Etruscan helmet with a typical high crest. Interestingly, a figure such as this could easily have been made in medieval Africa or in 20th-century Europe.

We also know what the earliest houses in Rome looked like because small models of them (left) were made to hold the ashes of the dead.

Arts and crafts

The Etruscans had a strong influence on Roman civilization. Although we do not understand the Etruscan language yet, we do know that many Roman customs, and even Roman gods, were borrowed from them. The Etruscans were also one channel through which influences from Greece and the East arrived in Italy. Etruscan craftsmanship was exceptional, especially in metalwork (Etruria was well known for its rich mineral resources), and included intricate and costly jewelry.

This clay figure wearing a tartan robe (left) came from a grave in the Etruscan city of Caere (now Cerveteri). It dates from the late seventh century B.C. No one knows the meaning of the movement he is making with his hands.

The founder of Rome

According to Roman myth, Rome was founded by Romulus, son of the god of war, Mars. As babies, Romulus and his twin brother Remus were left to die. They were rescued by a she-wolf and brought up by shepherds. When they had grown up, they founded the city. But they quarreled over who should rule it, and Romulus killed Remus. This bronze she-wolf (right) is Etruscan and was made about 500 B.C. The twins were added about 2,000 years later.

The City of Rome

Rome, "the Eternal City," has been at the heart of European history for more than 2,000 years. Once a group of small villages clustered on seven hills, it became a republic in 509 B.C. As its territory expanded, the city thrived and grew, but after the long civil wars of the first century B.C., the elected officials of the republic were replaced by emperors. Under Augustus, the first emperor, and his successors, Rome became both the largest and the grandest city that Europe had ever seen. Many cities and towns across the Empire became smaller models of Rome and Roman civilization.

The emperor Augustus (above), whose long reign (27 B.C.–A.D. 14) established imperial rule. He holds a standard bearing the imperial eagle.

The Roman Forum

The Forum was the chief public square in Rome. In early times, it was the center of religion, trade (there were shops all around), business, political affairs, and even gladiator fights. Gradually, it became more grand. The storekeepers moved out and monumental buildings sprang up (below).

Police and fire services

Augustus established a paramilitary force against riots and disorders, but most policing was done by ordinary people. Neighbors would combine against a troublemaker. Fire was a constant danger in the crowded city, and Augustus also set up a body of firefighters, but they could not prevent the fire of A.D. 64 from burning for six days.

Republic and Empire

The Roman Republic was not really democratic, because the patricians (nobles) held the real power. The Romans disliked the idea of rule by a king, and Augustus called himself not "emperor" but "first citizen." He also kept the institutions and officials of the Republic, though they no longer held much power.

Public speaking was an important skill in Rome, and lawyers and politicians were skilled orators.

Coins minted in Rome. Left: The Roman eagle, bird of Jupiter. Right: The double-faced Janus, god of gateways, who looks both ways.

A coin of the Roman Republic (right) which shows a citizen casting his vote in an election.

Senate

Patricians (members of noble families) were represented in the Senate, which was the chief power under the Republic. Originally, the Senate had 300 members; later it had 600. The two elected consuls, who headed the government, were also patricians, until plebs were admitted as consuls in 366 B.C. Under the emperors, the Senate lost much of its power in government, though it did retain some influence.

The plebs

The common people, called plebs in the early Republic, were not all poor. Some were quite wealthy, but not of noble birth. Under the Republic, the plebs struggled for greater rights against the dominant patricians, or nobles, who were big landowners. They had some success, gaining their own assembly, their own officials, and equal treatment in law.

This map shows Rome at its greatest extent, about A.D. 300. The surrounding wall was 32 miles (51.5 km) long, and the Tiber River was crossed by six bridges. The Colosseum appears in the center, and below it, imperial palaces and the Circus Maximus.

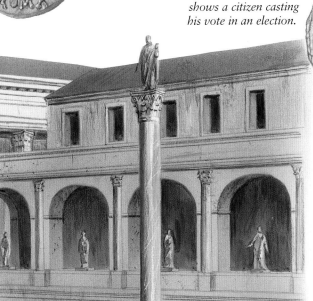

Law and justice

The greatest strength of the Roman Empire, after its armies, was its law. Not even the emperor was above the law, and the rights of citizens were firmly upheld in the courts. The Christian apostle Paul escaped a sentence of flogging because he was a Roman citizen. Then, as today, cases in court were decided by argument between lawyers, and judgments by elected magistrates were based on earlier decisions.

Shops and Markets

As Rome expanded, so did its shops and markets. Shops lined the main streets, while high-class craftsmen such as goldsmiths could be found in the oldest commercial center, the Roman Forum. The biggest shopping complex was the huge, covered Market of Trajan, built about A.D. 110. As well as market stalls, it had five stories of shops. On the ground floor were the sellers of fruit and flowers. The second story was made up of spacious vaulted halls, where oil and wine could be stored in large quantities. The shops on the next two floors sold food, including herbs and spices, and the fourth story held welfare offices where free food was given out. On the top floor were fish tanks, some supplied with fresh water from an aqueduct and others filled with sea water from the coast.

A shop

Shops such as this (below) could be found on the streets of any Roman town. They were often self-contained rooms in a house, rented from the owners. The staircase in the background leads to the living quarters of the proprietor and his—or sometimes her—family. More successful shopkeepers had their own house elsewhere.

Producers and buyers

In early times, most of the goods sold in the shops of a Roman town were produced by the same people who sold them. As time went by, and Rome grew into a city of one million people, a wholesale business developed. Middlemen controlled more and more of the trade—they bought up all the produce of the growers or craftspeople and sold it to stores.

Shopping

Rich people sent their slaves to do the shopping, and in Rome they probably visited the market on most days. Elsewhere, markets operated once a week. Poorer people did their own shopping, and, as most of them had no kitchens, they bought a lot of ready-cooked food. They could not afford expensive food and bought mainly bread (straight from the oven), a kind of porridge, and filling vegetables such as beans and lentils.

Meat

Butchers sold a great variety of meats, perhaps more than we can get from our butchers and supermarkets today. Meat included pork, mutton, goat, beef, wild boar, rabbit, geese, and various other birds, as well as dormice that were specially bred to be eaten. The Romans also ate parts of animals that might seem strange to us—sow's udder, for example, was a great delicacy.

Bakeries

Flour was milled from grain (left) and was rather coarse compared with the flour we have today. As a result, Roman bread was probably chewier than ours and the dough did not rise so well. Bread was usually baked in the baker's shop, and many bakers milled their own flour.

The scene on a busy street. It is early in the day and some of the goods are still arriving, but already there are shoppers out on the street. Later in the day, the scene would have been more hectic. The government in Rome often passed regulations to prevent tradesmen from taking over the streets.

Above: Bakers took their hot loaves out of the oven with a long-handled spatula, as in this decorative mosaic.

Below: A female innkeeper discusses the bill with a departing traveler. The most expensive item was for female company.

Inside a tavern

Taverns ranged from dark and dirty drinking dens to reasonable restaurants. They usually had a stone counter near the front, with large jars of wine and water (wine was diluted before drinking). In the rear, there were stoves and space to prepare food. Often there was also another more private room at the back, and sometimes a courtyard.

Inns and Taverns

Rome and the Roman Empire had several kinds of taverns, which provided food and drink, and inns, which also offered a bed for the night. Both also offered entertainment of various kinds, most of it illegal or at least not respectable, such as gambling. Inns and taverns were often situated near the public baths and markets. Few respectable Romans, and certainly no respectable women, entered a tavern unless they had to. In the eyes of the law, a person who kept a tavern was not much better than a criminal. However, there were some better inns, or hotels, for upper-class travelers, such as ambassadors and imperial officials, with no other place to stay.

A sign advertising food and drink, from one of many taverns in the port of Ostia that catered to sailors, traders, and others passing through.

This mosaic shows an argument over a game of dice. Gambling peaked in the annual springtime festival of Saturnalia, when all rules were relaxed for a week.

Gambling

Taverns in Rome usually had a room at the back for gambling, though there were laws against it. A tavern keeper could not be prosecuted for allowing gambling on his premises, but neither could he sue violent customers who caused damage under the influence of heavy losses or strong wine (or both). Some gamblers cheated, and archeologists have found loaded dice.

Eating out

Well-to-do Romans did not go out to eat. Feasts and parties were held at home. In town or in the country, and usually when traveling, they could stay with friends, or friends of friends. Hospitality to strangers was a well-established custom, and for people who had plenty of money and slaves, entertaining visitors was no great chore. If they had nowhere else to stay when traveling far from home, wealthy people stayed at the best inns and often had their food prepared by their own slaves, using the hotel's kitchens.

Takeout

Taverns usually had a few simple tables and benches for those who wanted to eat there. Most customers took the food home to eat.

Left: Simple sandals such as these were provided by the management to protect bathers' feet.

❶ OPEN AIR SWIMMING POOL
❷ MAIN ENTRANCE
❸ TEPIDARIUM (WARM ROOM)
❹ APODYTERIUM (CHANGING ROOM), WHERE CLOTHES WERE LEFT

This section of a mosaic (left) shows women exercising. Women (and children as well) went to the baths at a different time from the men, or went to their own special baths.

This mosaic (right) from the Baths of Caracalla shows a judge umpiring a game.

Exercise and games

Most Romans visited the baths once a day, in the late afternoon. Exercise came first, to work up a sweat. This might be weight-lifting, using dumbbells (like the woman above), jogging (some baths had a running track), boxing, wrestling, or playing ball games. Women often exercised by rolling a hoop.

Washing

In the usual procedure, the customers first entered the warm, steamy room called the calidarium. Here, attendants rubbed bathers' bodies with olive oil and then scraped them clean using a strigil. The bathers would then cool off slowly in the tepidarium, take a quick plunge into the cold frigidarium, and perhaps go swimming in the open air pool.

❺ CALIDARIUM (HOT AND STEAMY)—A "DRY BATH." THE TOP OF THE DOME COULD BE OPENED FOR VENTILATION.

❻ FRIGIDARIUM (COLD WATER ROOM)

❼ GYMNASIUM, FOR VIGOROUS EXERCISE

Keeping warm

Public baths had an ingenious heating system. Air was heated in a furnace and then flowed under the floor and through vents in the walls. The temperature could be raised or lowered in different rooms. In some places, such as the Aquae Sulis (Bath) in Britain, hot springs were used.

Some instruments used at the baths—sponges and an oil flask were attached to metal strigils for scraping oil, sweat, and dirt from the skin.

The Baths

Even the smallest Roman town had public baths. Rome itself had hundreds, mostly free, including the huge Baths of Caracalla, which was a magnificent palace of marble and mosaics that covered 27 acres (11 h). Although the Romans believed in keeping their bodies fit and clean, the baths were not just for bathing or swimming. They were more like combined sports and leisure complexes, and were the center of social life.

Women

Roman women had more freedom than women in many earlier civilizations. Although the Romans believed that a woman's place was in the home, women still took part in social life both with and without their husbands. Well-born women did not need to have jobs or take part in public life. There were female workers, traders, even gladiators, but they were mostly either slaves or freed women (former slaves).

A woman pours scent into a scent bottle, from a wall painting in a Roman house.

Rights of women

Initially, women were regarded as the property of their husbands or fathers, but in time, upper-class women gained many legal rights. They could manage their own money and business affairs, and their rights to own property were stronger than those of English women 150 years ago. Some lower-class women worked with their husbands, especially in skilled crafts.

Clothing

Women wore loose-fitting tunics. A woman's main garment was the ankle-length stola, tied at the waist and below the breasts and worn over a shift or petticoat. Sometimes women wore a cloak (palla) on top. It was a rectangle of cloth, usually draped over one shoulder and around the back, with the other end carried over the arm. It could also be pulled over the head. Most women wore sandals on their feet.

A necklace of mother-of-pearl and emeralds, a gold snake bracelet, and a portrait ring.

Clothes were usually made of wool, sometimes linen, with silk for the rich.

Hairstyles

Upper-class women grew their hair long but wore it piled up on the head in different ways. Hairstyles were very elaborate and often took a long time to create and arrange. They sometimes included artificial hair and a wire framework for special effects. Fashionable styles changed as often then as they do now.

Jewelry

Roman women wore jewelry very similar to the kinds that women wear today—mainly necklaces, bracelets, rings, and earrings (they had pierced ears). For the rich, jewelry was made of gold and gems, and even diamonds from India. Poorer women wore cheaper jewelry made of glass and colored stones set in brass.

This ivory comb was found in a grave. The letters spell out the words "Modestina, Vale" ("Farewell, Modestina").

Marriage

By the second century A.D., relations between husbands and wives were based on affection, not just obedience. They were partners. Fathers no longer ordered the death of unwanted babies, or chose their daughters' husbands. A Roman wedding was much more like a modern Christian wedding, with gold rings and bridesmaids. Another part of a Roman wedding was the sacrifice of a pig or sheep.

A nursemaid and a mother give a baby a bath.

Ladies of leisure

As they did not go out to work and had many slaves to do the housework, upper-class women seem to have had easy lives. In fact, they had plenty to do—managing the household, bringing up the children, organizing the family's social life, not to mention dressing up!

Motherhood

A woman's most important job was bringing up children. The emperor gave awards to good mothers because they played an important part in young children's education. Boys were often very close to their mothers, but more distant from their fathers. We have fewer resources about mothers and daughters (perhaps because all the records we have were written by men).

Cosmetics

Well-born women used many cosmetics made from plants, insects, shellfish, and other natural materials. These cosmetics were made at home. Some of them were dangerous to a woman's health—at one time it was fashionable to use a white face makeup that was made with powdered white lead mixed with oil. This was very bad for the skin. The woman standing at the right in this picture is a trained cosmetician.

Attendants

There were far more slaves than citizens in the Roman Empire, including household attendants. A lady getting dressed might be attended by four or five female maids. Slaves were property—they could be bought and sold—but household slaves were usually well treated and they could often gain or buy their freedom.

Children

The Romans treated children as if they were small, but unreliable, adults. Boys were thought old enough to marry at 14, and girls at 12. Children wore the same kind of clothes as adults, and girls in rich families had complicated hairstyles like their mothers. In early times, a Roman father had been like a dictator, and could have had his children killed or sold into slavery. But by the second century A.D., that was illegal (although children from very poor families were probably still sold), and family life was based on affection. The statesman Cicero said that a good father should be respected by his children. Some fathers were criticized for spoiling their children, especially sons, who grew into selfish adults.

A charm in the form of a gold pendant, called a bulla, was worn by free-born Roman boys and girls to keep evil spirits away. Poorer children wore leather ones.

Games and toys

Well-off Romans had plenty of time for sports and play. Popular games included "Robbers," which was like a simple form of chess, and a board game called "Twelve Lines," which was like backgammon. Archeologists have found a huge variety of toys, including marbles, wooden and cloth dolls, carved animals, dolls' houses, rocking horses, and toys on wheels. Boys liked imitating chariot races with toy chariots.

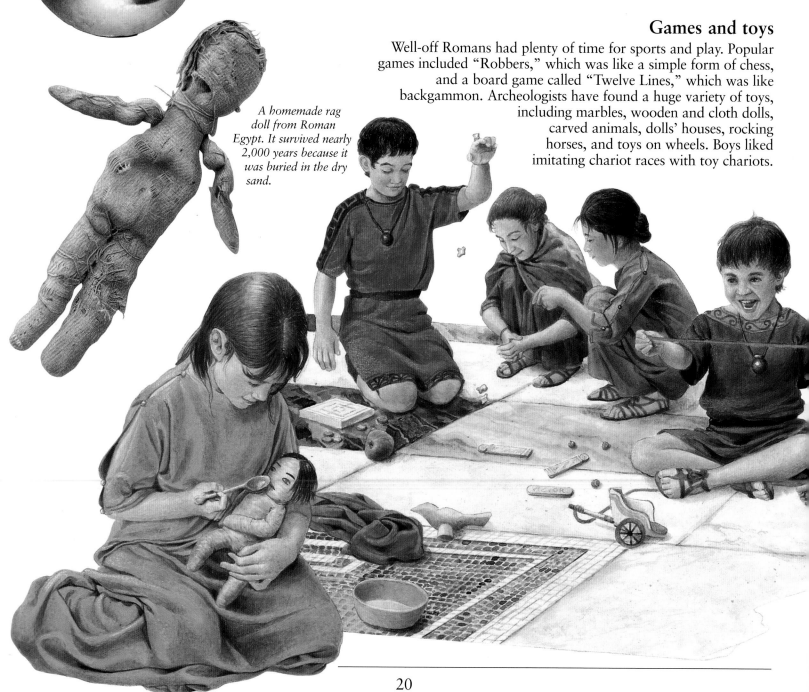

A homemade rag doll from Roman Egypt. It survived nearly 2,000 years because it was buried in the dry sand.

Education

Well-off boys, and sometimes girls, went to their first school at the age of seven. Their education was mostly learning things by heart, and teachers often used the cane on their students. Some Romans were not happy with this system and complained about it. A small number of students went on to higher education, mostly studying literature, and boys finished at a school of rhetoric, which taught public-speaking skills. A few from top families might then have visited the cities of Greece, which the Romans regarded as the heart of learning.

Above: A boy's first teacher was his father, although in later times he usually had a tutor, who was often an educated slave.

Pets

Most Roman households had guard dogs. Collar tags have been found that give the name and address of the owner. Richer children had many pets. Birds were popular, including songbirds such as nightingales.

This young slave is probably already an experienced waiter.

Reading and writing

Those who had a full education could read and write in both Latin (the Romans' native language) and Greek. "Books" were in the form of scrolls, and were very rare because they had to be copied by hand. The form of paper they were written on was also expensive because it was made either from papyrus reeds imported from Egypt or from the skins of newborn lambs (vellum).

Slave children

Some owners had the children of their household slaves properly educated, but for most slaves, from an early age, life consisted only of work. They did not necessarily have a family life because they belonged not only to their parents but also to their owners. Still, there is a character in many Roman stories called the "crafty slave"—he was cleverer than his owners, whether or not he was educated.

Ink was made from soot; pens from reeds or metal. The instrument on the right of the pen is a bronze stylus, used for writing on reusable wax tablets at school or home.

Building and Technology

The Romans did not produce such great thinkers and artists as their forerunners, the ancient Greeks. But in practical affairs—such as building and engineering—they were far superior. When it came to building roads, bridges, or sewers, or making machines and tools, no other people in Europe reached the standards set by the Romans until well over a thousand years after the Roman Empire had disappeared.

A crane being used on a monumental building, first century A.D.

Engineering

Although the Romans lacked artificial engines to provide power, they had animals (oxen and horses) and a huge supply of manpower (slaves). Tread-wheels, bigger versions of the wheels that modern pet hamsters like to play in, provided the power to pump water from deep mines or to operate lifting devices (such as the one above).

The design of the Pantheon, to which the emperor Hadrian himself probably contributed, shows a skillful sense of space. The diameter of the dome is exactly the same as the distance between the top of the dome and the floor—a huge ball would fit exactly inside. This vast circular space is lit by a single great round window at the top of the dome.

The Pantheon

The Pantheon ("temple to all the gods") is the finest surviving building from ancient Rome. It was built by the cultured emperor Hadrian in 118–125. (The porch on the left is a century older than this.) The dome is an amazing 142 feet (43.3 m) in diameter, and its construction was probably made possible by the Roman invention of concrete. It remained the largest dome in the world until the 20th century.

Roman roads were so well made that some still exist. The Appian Way (left) was the main road leading south from Rome.

Underneath the city streets lead pipes carried fresh water and, at a deeper level, sewers carried away waste from lavatories. Houses not connected to the sewer system had cess pits.

Plumbing

Roman water supply and drains were superior to anything in Europe until the 19th century. In the city, fresh water was carried in lead or pottery pipes to public wells, fountains, and baths, and also to the houses of wealthy residents. As far as possible, water was moved by gravity; for example, a raised tank would operate a fountain. Pipes were fitted with valves to prevent water running the wrong way.

Roads

The famous Roman roads were built by the army, as straight as possible, for troops to move around the empire quickly. They were equally useful to traders and other travelers. Materials varied, but there was usually a deep foundation of small stones with heavy slabs on top. They were lined by kerbstones, and the surface sloped down from the center so the rain ran off.

Water power

When the wheat harvest was gathered, the grains of corn were taken to a mill, such as the one here. Water from a river or stream was channeled through to the mill, where it flowed over a water wheel. As the force of the falling water turned the wheel, it made power to turn grindstones. Grain was crushed between the stones, and this is how flour was made.

Bridges

Unlike the Greeks, whose architecture was all straight lines (the "post and beam" method), the Romans developed the arch (and the dome). The arch allowed the Romans to span wide spaces with their bridges and aqueducts, many of which are still standing today. Aqueducts carried fresh water to towns from springs high in the hills, sometimes many miles away.

The Milvian Bridge north of Rome was built about 100 B.C. It carried the Via Vlaminia, the main road to Etruria.

❶ MASTS TO SUPPORT
RIGGING FOR THE AWNING
❷ AWNING
❸ TOP TIER OF SEATS RESERVED FOR WOMEN
❹ TRAPDOORS ALLOWED FOR SUDDEN APPEARANCES
❺ SANDY FLOOR TO SOAK UP BLOOD

Vespasian

The emperor Vespasian (A.D. 69–79) was a popular general who was made emperor by his troops. He built the Colosseum, although it was not finished until after his death. His family name was Flavius, and the Colosseum was originally called the Flavian Amphitheater. The games held there lasted all day, sometimes for several days in a row. People could attend for free, as the emperor paid the huge costs. The games had a political purpose. As well as making the emperor popular, they allowed Rome's unruly people to let off steam. This made them less likely to start riots or revolts.

The building

The Colosseum is a masterpiece of design. The huge weight of the stone benches is supported by arches, which form galleries running behind the seats. The complicated network of staircases, ramps, arcades, and passageways was reached by 76 separate entrances, all numbered. Unseen, below ground level, was a maze of rooms and passages, including animal pens and quarters for the gladiators.

The Colosseum

Every Roman town had an amphitheater, a large stadium where popular entertainments were staged. The largest was the Colosseum in Rome, which was built about A.D. 70–80 and replaced an earlier wooden building. An oval arena surrounded by seating, it measured 617 by 512 feet (188 x 165 m), and was 157 feet (48 m) high. It held about 50,000 spectators. The seats could be covered by a gigantic awning for protection against the sun. Roughly half of the building still stands in the middle of modern Rome, and it is the most impressive building in the city.

A coin of the emperor Titus (A.D. 79–81), which shows the Colosseum as it was when first built. The top story, above the three rows of arches, is hung with shields.

Right: With shin guards but bare chests, gladiators' armor was flashy rather than useful.

There were many kinds of gladiators. This is the helmet of a so-called "heavily armed" gladiator (hoplomachus), but his upper body might be unprotected like the clay figures above.

Gladiators

Most gladiators were slaves, including prisoners of war, and criminals. They were trained at gladiator schools, but their lives were short, as they usually fought to the death. However, a successful gladiator could win his freedom, and big prize money as well. Some became popular heroes, and a few gladiators were volunteers. Professional gladiators may have sometimes used their skills to "fix" their fights, just as TV wrestlers do now.

The games were so popular that they were often the subject of decoration in Roman houses. The mosaic below shows different types of gladiators, including a "net man" (retiarius), whose weapons were a net (to entangle his opponent) and a trident (top right).

Animal fights were popular. This gladiator is armed and stands a chance against the leopard. Condemned criminals had their hands tied, and were simply torn to pieces.

Blood and death

The Romans called their entertainments "games" but they consisted mainly of fights between gladiators and public executions of criminals. Blood and cruelty—the torture of humans and animals—was what the Roman crowd liked to see. This may seem disgusting (as some Romans thought it was), but some people today also enjoy watching extreme violence and cruelty, though on TV and film.

DOROTHY LYNAS

Circus and Theater

The Romans' favorite sport was chariot-racing. The race track called Circus Maximus was one of the oldest buildings in Rome. It was close to the emperor's palace, from which an underground tunnel led to his private box.

Chariot racing

Racing was a highly professional sport. Riders belonged to different teams, with their own colors, patrons, fans, and staff of trainers, vets, blacksmiths, and carpenters. The charioteers were often slaves at first and could buy their freedom with their prize money. One champion, named Scorpus, won 2,000 races and was a rich man when he died in a crash at age 27.

The theater

Early Roman theaters (right) were temporary wooden buildings. Stone theaters were built after 55 B.C. They had permanent architectural sets, a raised stage, and tiers of seats in a half circle. Audiences liked comedies best, and these were mostly based on Greek plays.

Actors and masks

Actors had a low status in society. Most were slaves, or former slaves. They wore masks with exaggerated expressions (left) to represent the type of character that they were playing. The same actor could play several different parts by wearing different masks.

Roman drama

There were few Roman playwrights to compare with the Greeks. The best of the few whose work has survived was Seneca, and he wrote his plays to be read rather than performed. By A.D. 200, drama had almost disappeared and was replaced by crude variety performances and wild animal shows.

Chariots were very light and were drawn by four horses. They raced up and down the Circus Maximus seven times, and the sharp turns at each end caused frequent accidents.

Soldiers

The basis of the Roman Empire was the Roman army, the first truly professional army of volunteer citizens in history. The legionaries (a legion contained up to 5,000 men) signed on for 20 years. Apart from fighting, the main job of the legionaries was guarding the frontiers of the Empire, and many of them never saw Italy. As a result, they came to feel greater loyalty to their own generals than to the distant emperor. This became a problem when rival generals, supported by their own men, fought for the imperial throne.

Armor

In the first to second centuries A.D., Roman soldiers wore a metal helmet and armor breastplate, and they carried a shield that protected them from neck to knee. Jointed plates, mounted on leather strips, allowed free movement of the shoulders. Chain mail, made of metal links, was worn earlier. Auxiliary troops (allies of the Romans or men who fought for pay) wore their own kind of armor.

The emperor Hadrian (117–138) decided the Empire was big enough and set about creating frontiers that could be defended easily. One result was Hadrian's Wall in northern Britain, which ran across the country south of modern Scotland. It had a fort every mile, with two watchtowers between each fort. Larger forts, such as the one shown here (left), provided back-up.

Each legion carried a decorated pole, called a standard, into battle. To lose the standard was considered a disgrace.

A Roman foot soldier's chief weapon in hand-to-hand fighting was the short sword. He also carried a spear. The steel blade of this sword has rusted, but the gold and silver hilt has survived undamaged.

Forts

Wherever a legion was stationed, it built its own fort, following the standard plan, in the shape of a triangle. It was surrounded by a stone-and-earth wall with towers at each corner and two more guarding the four gates. The main buildings were barracks for the troops, houses for the officers, and a large house at the center for the general. Also included were offices, stables, stores, workshops, baths, hospitals, and a prison.

The Romans invented a variety of machines for attacking enemy towns. This siege tower (left), with soldiers inside, could be pushed up to the walls where the soldiers jumped out to attack the defenders.

The Praetorian Guard

These were elite troops, originally the emperor's bodyguards, who were paid three times as much as ordinary legionaries. They were stationed on the outskirts of Rome, so they could act fast in case of a serious riot. They came to have a dangerous influence on politics in the late second century A.D. In fact, in A.D. 193 they killed the emperor and offered the job to whoever would pay them the most.

An attack on a town. In a siege, it was often unnecessary to do any fighting. The attackers would build their own fortifications around the town and wait for hunger or disease to force the defenders to surrender.

Elephants frightened an enemy who had never seen them before, but they were not useful against experienced soldiers. A few well-aimed arrows or spears made them panic, often causing more trouble for their own side than for the enemy.

The Punic Wars

By 264 B.C., the Roman Republic had conquered its neighbors in mainland Italy and wanted to conquer Sicily as well. But Sicily was also claimed by Carthage, in North Africa. Rome's three wars against Carthage are known as the Punic Wars and went on for more than a century, from 264 to 146 B.C. They ended with the complete destruction of Carthage.

Hannibal crossed the Alps with elephants, though only one survived to carry him through Italy. The Romans also used elephants during the conquest of Britain in A.D. 43.

Hannibal

During the Second Punic War (218–201 B.C.), the great Carthaginian general Hannibal invaded Italy from Spain. He crossed the Alps in winter and took the Romans by surprise. He remained in Italy for 13 years. The Romans could not defeat him, but Hannibal was unable to capture Rome. In the end, the Romans sent an army to North Africa. Hannibal had to return to defend Carthage, and he was defeated.

Vestal virgins

Vesta, a sister of Juno, was associated with the prosperity of the Roman state. Her circular shrine (below) was in the Roman Forum, and she was served by the Vestal Virgins, who were Rome's only priestesses. Daughters of noble families, they were chosen as young girls and each served for 30 years, keeping Vesta's permanent flame alight.

Sacrifices and offerings

Roman religion included complicated ceremonies in which offerings such as wine and incense were made and an animal was sacrificed. The animal was first sprinkled with salted flowers prepared by the Vestal Virgins. Afterwards, its insides were examined by special priests who could foretell the intentions of the gods by "reading" the liver.

Religion

The chief Roman god was Jupiter, who headed a family of gods and goddesses. Eventually they became identified with the gods of ancient Greece—Jupiter with the Greek Zeus, his wife Juno with her Greek equivalent, Hera, and so on. Worship and sacrifices were carried out to please the gods. As time went by, the Romans adopted a number of foreign gods and cults. Roman religion was closely linked with politics. Although Julius Caesar was an atheist, he held the role of chief priest.

The imperial cult

Augustus, the first Roman emperor, understood the political importance of religion. He encouraged the idea that the emperor himself was divine or semi-divine. Dissatisfied subjects were less likely to rebel against a god! Emperor-worship never became a true religion, but it was a strong cult in some parts. The emperor Commodus (above) insisted that the Senate call him a god and identified himself with the mythical hero Hercules, who wore a lion-skin cloak.

Household gods

Household gods, penates, and manes (spirits of dead ancestors) were worshiped in the home. Most families had a little shrine in the atrium. There were other minor gods or spirits, such as the lares (right), who inhabited a particular place. Their shrines could often be seen at crossroads.

Above: This wall painting shows Bacchus, god of wine, dressed in a cloak of grapes with his attendant panther. He was identified with the formidable Greek god Dionysus, whose worship included extravagant mystical rites.

Right: This decorative bronze statue shows Fortuna, the Roman goddess of luck or good fortune. She was the focus of several cults in later times. Among other things, she was believed to help women who wanted to have children.

Mithraism

Mithraism, which came from Iran, was a macho religion that became popular among soldiers. Mithras was part sun-god and part hero. He was worshiped in dim cells or caves that were most unlike the great temples of the Roman gods. But Mithraism did not admit women, and therefore Christianity proved more successful.

Worshipers of Mithras believed that all life on Earth sprang from the blood of a bull slain by the hero-god before he went to heaven.

The sistrum (below), a kind of musical rattle, was used by the priests of the Egyptian goddess Isis—hers was one of the most popular mystery cults in Rome. The sistrum's sound was believed to drive away evil spirits.

Mystery cults

The liveliest religions in the Roman Empire were the foreign "mystery cults." Roman rulers were suspicious of them. They feared that they might be a cover for treason, but usually tolerated them. The worship of Cybele, the "Great Mother," originated in Anatolia (Turkey) and was popular with women. Her worship included music and dancing, and this carving (above) of one of her priests shows instruments used to worship her.

Christianity

Christianity was founded at roughly the same time as the Roman Empire. Christians, however, refused to worship the Roman gods, which was a kind of treason. Most emperors ignored them as far as was possible, but sometimes they were hunted down and killed, especially in the third century. Yet Christianity gained more and more believers. In 313, the religion was granted official toleration, and the emperor Constantine (306–337) made it the chief Roman religion.

After 313, when the edict of Milan granted tolerance to Christianity, Christians were free to build their own churches (right). They copied the type of Roman building called a basilica, which was a long hall divided by rows of columns.

A Roman House

Wealthy Romans were very rich indeed. They often owned a country estate as well as a town house. Although they lacked modern services such as electricity, living conditions were very comfortable thanks to their many servants (actually slaves). Houses followed a traditional pattern, although this varied in different parts of the Empire. From the outside, only a few tiny windows high up on the walls were visible. The main rooms were grouped around the atrium, an open courtyard in the center. Country houses, or villas, were usually attached to a large estate or farm. Town houses were grouped in the fashionable parts of a town. In Rome itself, only the very rich could afford to own them.

Above: A small oven made of stone. A charcoal fire kept the food in the upper part warm. Main kitchen stoves were larger, with a flat top where soup could be boiled or meat grilled.

The private house

Houses of stone or brick, sometimes plastered, were usually built on one floor. Especially in Rome, where space was limited, some might have had an upper floor. Some had a basement, a maze of small rooms where the slaves lived.

Decoration

Although rooms were sparsely furnished, they were richly decorated with paintings, carvings, and mosaics. Often, all the walls were covered with paintings of abstract patterns or realistic pictures, or panels of different colors, while the floor was covered in mosaics. Mosaics are pictures made by arranging small cubes of different-colored stone or glass, although glass was not used for floor mosaics. Mosaics were often designed in geometric black and white patterns.

❶ *ROOFS WERE GENERALLY COVERED WITH FLAT AND HOOPED TILES.*

❷ *SOMETIMES ROOMS WERE RENTED OUT AND ROOMS ON THE STREET WERE OFTEN TURNED INTO SHOPS. CUSTOMERS DID NOT HAVE TO ENTER THE SHOP BECAUSE THE COUNTER WAS RIGHT AT THE FRONT.*

❸ *BEDROOMS WERE USUALLY SMALL, AND FEW MEMBERS OF THE HOUSEHOLD HAD ONE OF THEIR OWN.*

❹ *MAIN ENTRANCE*

❺ *VESTIBULE, OR HALL*

❻ *SHOP*

Mosaic-makers became so skillful that it was hard to tell their pictures from paintings. This mosaic of doves comes from the emperor Hadrian's villa at Tivoli, near Rome. The villa was a country estate the size of a small town!

Furniture

Rich Romans often owned valuable and varied furniture, but to our eyes today their homes would look underfurnished. Large pieces, such as hefty wardrobes, were especially rare. Wealthy families often moved between town and country houses, and they liked furniture that could be moved from house to house or room to room. Although they had chairs and stools, the Romans preferred lounging on couches at mealtimes.

This double-ended bed (above) does not look comfortable, but it would have had a mattress, blankets, and pillows on top. Like the folding stool (below), it is made mainly of bronze. Furniture was a type of property and was regarded as an investment, so the wealthy often had furniture made of costly materials.

8 ROMANS LOVED THEIR GARDENS, WHICH HAD STATUES AND PERHAPS A POOL OR FOUNTAIN. ROOMS NEXT TO THE GARDEN, USUALLY INCLUDING THE DINING ROOM, ENJOYED NATURAL LIGHT AND A BEAUTIFUL VIEW.

Glass-making was one of the finest crafts, and the houses of rich people might contain glass vessels (above) made in places as far away as Syria and western Germany. Silver jugs, bowls, and wine cups were also made in different countries. They were more durable than glass, and, in times of need, they could be melted down for money.

9 THE PERISTYLE WAS A ROOFED COLONNADE AROUND A GARDEN.

10 THE DINING ROOM HAD COUCHES AROUND THREE WALLS. PEOPLE ATE OFF SMALL PORTABLE TABLES. IF THERE WERE MANY GUESTS, THEY MOVED INTO THE PERISTYLE OR ATRIUM.

Right: A sculpture of a child playing with a wig. Sculptures, made of bronze or marble, were more often placed in the garden and open spaces rather than in closed rooms.

11 THE ATRIUM WAS THE CENTER OF THE MAIN PART OF THE VILLA WHERE THE HOUSEHOLD GODS WERE KEPT. RAINWATER FELL THROUGH THE OPEN SKYLIGHT INTO A POOL IN THE FLOOR AND DRAINED INTO A TANK.

Running the household

A wealthy household, which usually included relatives such as elderly grandparents, or sometimes visitors, required a full-time manager. This was the job of the owner's wife. She gave the slaves their daily orders, looked after young children, and made sure that the household ran smoothly.

12 THE KITCHEN WAS QUITE SMALL. IT HAD A STOVE AND A SINK. THE LAVATORY WAS NEARBY, SO THAT IT COULD BE FLUSHED WITH THE USED WASHING-UP WATER.

Farming

The best and most useful way for a gentleman to make his living, said Cicero (106–43 B.C.), was as a farmer. He should have said "landowner" because the sort of farmer he meant had laborers and slaves to do the work. Farming was the most important occupation in the Roman Empire and, as the basis of the Empire's wealth, was even more important than trade. We think of the Romans as city people, but far more "citizens" lived in the country than in the towns. Farm sizes varied greatly. Early on, most were fairly small and run by families, but increasingly these were bought to form part of much larger estates.

Above: A small silver figure of a shepherd. He carries a lamb on his back, with a heavy container to balance it.

Above: Picking apples. Besides apples and grapes, figs, pears, and pomegranates were common fruits. Later came peaches, apricots, and a few lemons—but no oranges.

Harvesting olives

Olives were one of the most important crops, especially for their oil, although they were also eaten as fruit. Olives will grow in soil too poor for cereals, and from the second century A.D., when Italy could no longer produce enough, thousands of acres of olive groves were planted in the North African provinces. Olives were harvested by hitting the trees' branches to knock the olives to the ground, and then they were loaded into baskets and carried to the olive press.

Right: Wagons such as these would have been seen over much of the Empire. They were mostly used on farm tracks, as many main roads were not well-suited to wheeled vehicles.

Farm transport

Although the Romans had horses, mules, and donkeys, for heavy loads they used oxen as draught animals (which made the beef very tough!). Farmers' carts and wagons were no different from those still used in parts of Europe today. Some may have been based on Celtic designs.

Honey

Sugar was unknown in Roman Europe. Honey was the chief sweetener. Like wine-making, the secrets of bee-keeping were understood long before the Roman Empire. Hives were made of pottery (or sometimes wood or other material) and were arranged in rows. Different types of honey were produced and different techniques were used in different places. Thyme-based honey from Attica (Greece) had a high reputation in Rome.

This plow (below) was simply a spike that broke up the ground for sowing. Later, the Romans adopted a Celtic type of plow, which was better, as it also turned the soil.

Animals

Sheep were kept mainly for their wool, but also for milk. The Romans made cheese from both sheep's and goats' milk. Some big farms experimented with selective breeding. Like sheep, pigs were easy to keep, as they could partly fend for themselves—but they did need to be guarded from thieves and predators. Beef was less popular than pork, and people preferred sheep's milk to that of cows. Cattle were raised as working animals and for leather, and donkeys did lighter farmwork. Chickens provided eggs and meat.

Above: Pork was the Romans' favorite meat, and pigs were kept all over the Empire. They were easy to feed in the winter, and in the summer they foraged in the woods.

Cereals

Rome's huge growth as a city meant that it soon depended on imports for its main food supplies. By about A.D. 100, the fertile North African provinces were "Rome's breadbasket." They produced thousands of tons of wheat every year. Other cereals included barley (used for brewing beer), oats, and rye. The Romans did not understand how to grow rice, but imported it from the East.

Below: Trampling grapes into juice to make wine. The heavy sticks assist the crushing and, like the linked hands, help to prevent the men from slipping.

Wine

Wine-making was an ancient art, and vineyards existed all over the Empire, even in Britain. Wine was the favorite Roman drink. After A.D. 100, Rome's wine mainly came from North Africa, Spain, and Greece. However, vines flourished in Italy. The finest vintage wine was grown on the slopes of Mount Vesuvius, and in earlier times, Italian growers had exported wine to northern Europe. Grapes were also grown for eating and for grape juice.

A Roman Kitchen

The Romans had fewer foods than we do (no potatoes or tomatoes), but they had a great variety all the same (and even some foods that we don't have, such as grilled mouse!). Their food was perhaps healthier too, without the chemicals and additives that we have today. If they could afford to, the Romans ate well. On country estates, nearly all the food was home produce, but in the crowded city of Rome, food supply was big business. The emperors made sure that the poorer classes were supplied with free bread. Otherwise, food was brought in by the many tradesmen. These included specialists such as the *peponarii*, who sold melons. There were fewer middlemen than now—the grocer grew the vegetables that he sold, and the fishmonger caught his own fish.

SMALL PAN

COLANDER

This pan and colander are just like those we use today, except that they are bronze, not steel.

WATER JUG

Cooking

Many houses did not have kitchens, so Romans ate a lot of takeout food. But in big houses and country villas, slaves did all the cooking and served the meals. There were many slaves working in such a kitchen, under a head chef, probably with a wine steward and other specialists.

Fresh fruit and vegetables were stored in baskets. Other food, including wine and olive oil, was stored in pots or jars (amphorae) of pottery.

Preparing a dinner party

Dinner parties of the rich, which began in the early afternoon, might have lasted many hours. These were often held outside. The upper-class custom of reclining to eat made it difficult to squeeze many guests into a dining room, unless they were in the emperor's palace. A small army of slaves prepared and served a variety of dishes, often starting with eggs and ending with fruit. Dishes such as meat and vegetables were served separately.

Utensils

Knives of various kinds were used in the kitchen, and table knives were used at meals for cutting meat. Wooden ladles and metal spoons were also used, but the Romans preferred to eat with their fingers. They did not have forks.

GRATER

Fine glassware, such as these flasks, was more fragile and costly than pottery. It was probably used for serving rather than storage.

SOUP POT

FENNEL SEEDS

ROSEMARY

BASIL

PARSLEY

STONE MORTAR AND PESTLE

ANISE

CUMIN

Food

Romans grew many vegetables, such as asparagus, cabbage, carrots, cucumbers, leeks, lettuce, onions, squash, peas, and beans. They probably used up to 100 different herbs and spices, some of which they grew and some that they gathered wild. They ate many different kinds of meat, fish, and game.

Baking

In the city, most people bought bread from a bakery, but houses with kitchens often had an oven. Long-handled trays, such as this one on the left, might have been used for baking smaller items inside very hot ovens.

Food was cooked over burners fed with charcoal or wood.

WATER STOVE

Fresh food

For Roman cooks, like all others before refrigerators were invented, keeping food fresh was a problem. Some houses may have had larders or pantries, others had cool cellars. The Mediterranean provided a rich variety of fish, but the difficulty of getting it fresh to a kitchen in Rome made it expensive. The reason for the popularity of the strong fish sauce called garum may have been that it disguised the flavor of food that was past its use-by date.

JARS FOR OLIVE OIL AND WINE

GRILL WITH PLACES FOR POTS ON THE BACK

Workers and Crafts

Below: Decorative mosaic. The tesserae could be as small as 0.04 inches (1 mm) square, so that the mosaic looked like a painting.

People in Rome were always complaining about the noise. The trouble was that Rome was a huge manufacturing city. The commotion came from hundreds of different crafts—from the clang of blacksmiths' hammers, the roar of glassblowers' furnaces, the shouts of the wagoners, and the rattle and thud of carts on cobbled streets. Thousands of workshops were scattered throughout the city, not confined to an industrial area like they often are today. There were other differences too—producers were also salespeople. The man who sold a knife was the same man who made it. Butchers and grocers were also farmers. Women could be found in many trades, but generally they were far outnumbered by the men.

Cloth

After food production, clothes and fabrics made up one of the biggest industries (including crafts such as spinning, weaving, and dyeing). Clothes were generally simple, but Romans liked bright colors, and weavers made exotic decorative fabrics from imported silk. The army was a major customer of the clothing industry.

Mosaics

Romans decorated their houses with wall paintings and mosaics. Mosaics are pictures or patterns made out of small pebbles, or cubes of differently colored stone or glass (tesserae), fitted together in a bed of mortar. Stone mosaics in black and white often covered floors. They were so popular that they were mass-produced; people could buy a ready-made mosaic panel to set in the floor.

Roman jewelers were experts at making cameos, small relief carvings in hard stone. Portraits were a popular subject.

Blacksmiths made iron tools and steel weapons. The Romans made wrought (hammered) iron, but not cast iron, which requires extreme heat to melt it.

Silver

Conquests of silver-mining regions in Spain and Asia brought large quantities of silver to Rome. Silversmiths worked it into plates by hammering, and decorated it with techniques similar to those used today. It was made into coins as well, and was sometimes gilded with gold leaf. Small silver statues and domestic silverware, especially cups, were found in the homes of the rich.

The silver cup, decorated with skeletons, warns that life is short. It belonged to a silver service containing 109 pieces.

Pottery

Pottery was made on a wheel and fired in a special kiln. Most potters specialized in a certain type. On the tables of the wealthy, the dinner service might be high-quality shiny red Samian ware, which would reflect the light from elaborately molded and colored oil lamps. Plain earthenware bowls and dishes were much more common. Pottery was also used by builders, especially for roof tiles.

Plates, bowls, and dishes came in many forms and were made from a range of materials.

Glass

Glass vessels were rare until glass-blowing was invented in the first century B.C. Before long, glassworks existed all over the Empire. It was even made in sheets for windows. Glass vessels could be decorated in several different ways, including using the cameo process. Some glassworkers were highly skilled, and, as we know from their surviving work, their glass was as beautiful as any made since.

In this scene, a slave is buying a new kitchen knife. Cooks' knives often had decorative handles of carved bone or ivory.

Apartment Blocks

The great mass of people in the cities lived in apartment blocks that could be up to six stories high. Some were attractive, but most were built with cheap materials and weak foundations. As many Romans complained, hardly a day passed without one collapsing somewhere. Cicero owned a block and said of it, "Even the mice have moved out." Fires were common and caused many deaths when people were caught on upper floors. Except on the ground floor, there were no services. Water had to be carried up the stairs using buckets.

Fine glassware (above) could be found in expensive apartments.

Higher living

By the second century A.D., some apartments were built for rich tenants. They were built of brick, and plastered. The better apartments roughly followed the usual plan for a Roman house, and the ground floor even had gardens. Unlike others, they had their own lavatory and kitchen. Their occupants could afford expensive furnishings.

❶ SHOPS OCCUPIED MANY STREET-LEVEL UNITS, AND SOME HAD MEZZANINES OR UPPER FLOORS.

❷ WALLS WERE GENERALLY VERY THIN, AND UNTIL THE FIRST CENTURY B.C., THEY WERE OFTEN MADE OF RUBBLE.

❸ SOME APARTMENTS HAD A BALCONY.

Owners and tenants

Apartment blocks were usually built as an investment. The builder might let the whole block to a tenant, who in turn rented out apartments to individual families. The owner could make more money if he just kept patching up a shaky block rather than rebuilding it. A fire would attract a rich speculator, hoping to buy the site cheap from the distressed owner. Then he would rebuild it and make a large profit from the rent.

Windows

Glass windows were rare for apartment blocks. Some windows were covered by grills, others had wooden shutters, but there was nothing to keep out the cold without blocking the light. Apart from unglazed windows, these blocks looked much like similar buildings in Italian towns today.

Right: An iron grill covering a window.

Heat and light

Apartment blocks tended to be cold in winter and hot in summer, especially on the upper floors. There was no artificial heating, except occasionally on the ground floor, although many people had small portable stoves. Artificial light came only from candles and oil lamps, which were obvious fire hazards. Unlike peasants living in the countryside, people in apartments had no fireplaces to gather around.

An earthenware oil lamp. With such poor means of lighting, Romans got up at dawn to make the most of daylight.

❹ WINDOWS WERE OFTEN LARGER THAN IN PRIVATE HOUSES, TO LET IN MORE LIGHT.

The Port of Ostia

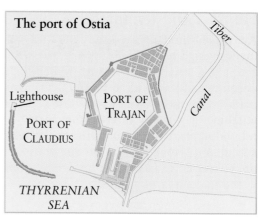

The port of Ostia

Ostia was a town on the coast at the mouth of the Tiber River, 15.5 miles (25 km) downstream from Rome. During the early Republic, it was a naval base, but it soon developed into a big commercial port and was later called Portus Romae, meaning "the port of Rome." By the time of the emperor Claudius (41–54), the river mouth was silting up, so a new harbor was built 1.8 miles (3 km) to the north. A huge ship, which had recently brought a stone obelisk from Egypt, was sunk in the harbor as a platform for a lighthouse. A small town developed there too, but Ostia remained the main center for business.

Above: The harbor of Claudius is shown to the left. It was far from perfect, and a storm in A.D. 62 destroyed 200 grain ships moored inside. The emperor Trajan (98–117) built a better-protected, five-sided harbor big enough for 300 ships. Canals connected it with the Tiber.

Big seagoing ships could not sail up the Tiber, and their cargo was transferred to river boats at Ostia. In this fragment of sculpture (left), a river boat is towed out to a merchant ship, and, on the right, merchant and captain celebrate a successful voyage.

Shipping

A typical merchant ship can be seen in the main picture below. It was made of wood, with a rounded hull and a single mast set amidships. A square sail hung from a yard attached to the mast, and the ship was steered with giant oars at the stern. Larger vessels might have two masts, or, like this one, a triangular jib sail on a bowsprit. Some big grain ships could carry up to 250 tons (228 t).

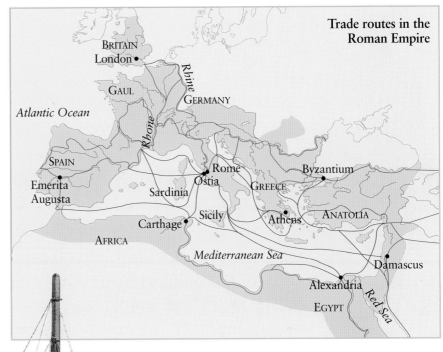

Trade routes in the
Roman Empire

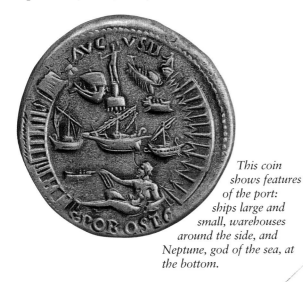

This coin shows features of the port: ships large and small, warehouses around the side, and Neptune, god of the sea, at the bottom.

Trade routes

Trading ships crisscrossed the Mediterranean. They sailed as far as Britain for tin and other metals. The main rivers, such as the Rhine and the Rhone, were also busy trade routes. Roads were built for the army, but traders also used them.

A busy scene in the port, with a cargo ship arriving, another behind preparing to leave, and the crew of a third (on the left) unfurling its sail. Behind are the warehouses, with a colonnade.

Right: In the market, a female stallholder is selling fruit to a slave.

Trade

In the early years of the Republic, the Romans exported goods and grew their food in the country surrounding Rome. By the second century B.C., they were importing almost everything, from all over the Empire and even beyond. Rome had no large industries and no mass production. Everything was made by hand. To supply one million people, however poor most of them were, all kinds of products (from food and cloth to pots and pans) had to be imported. Nearly all this trade traveled by water. Transporting goods in bulk overland was slow and expensive. Rome's huge imports arrived by sea and up the Tiber River.

Left: The fast-moving Mercury with wings, wearing boots and a helmet, was the god of traders. In this bronze he holds a purse of money. As messenger of the gods, he also carries his herald's staff.

Weights and measures

Gold and silver items were weighed on a simple balance, one half of which is shown above. Heavier objects were weighed on a steelyard. The object to be weighed was hung from a hook attached to a metal bar marked with a scale. A weight was moved along the bar until it was exactly horizontal. Then the weight could be read from the scale.

Bankers

Although Roman banks were not like ours and played a smaller part in everyday life, many banking services were available. A man could borrow money, though usually for a short time only and at high interest. He could make deposits, change currency (though Roman currency was accepted throughout the Empire), and operate on credit. Merchants borrowed money at interest to pay for cargo because if the ship was wrecked, the lender was the loser.

The standard Roman coin was the silver denarius. There was a gold coin worth 25 denarii, and smaller coins in bronze or copper. Roman coinage came to dominate the Mediterranean region, but many local currencies existed in the different provinces, keeping money changers very busy.

Below: A banker checks his calculations. Rich landowners sometimes offered interest-free loans to friends or clients. Professional moneylenders charged high interest, but they also took high risks.

Roman trade with China was irregular and small—only silk and some pottery such as this dish (right). Goods traveled overland on the Silk Road, passing through many hands on the way.

Merchant shipping

Merchant ships varied from small coasters (above) to vessels carrying hundreds of tons. They relied on square sails and oars, including steering oars (because they had no rudder). Merchants usually sailed their ships close to the coast, if they could, and preferred to spend nights in port. Shipwrecks were not uncommon (more than 1,000 have been found by divers in recent years). Pirates were also a menace.

This beautiful glass amphora, with its stand (right), was found near the seaside town of Pompeii (the town was buried by volcanic eruption in A.D. 79). Objects such as this had to be imported, and were expensive.

Luxury trade

Rich people in the Roman Empire, although few in number compared with the masses of poor people, were extremely rich. They could afford Chinese silk, Indian jewels, rare perfumes, silver, fine glassware, works of art, and exotic foods. Julius Caesar banned purple clothes because of the enormous cost of the dye, which came from Tyre. It was made from a type of shellfish, and tens of thousands of them were needed to make enough dye for just one toga.

Left: A scrap of relief sculpture from southern Germany shows an oar-powered ship heavily laden with barrels of wine.

Exotic animals

Some traders made big profits by importing wild animals for the "games." In the emperor Trajan's games of A.D. 107, held to celebrate a recent victory, 11,000 animals were killed in a few days. This was big business. Lions, tigers, rhinoceroses, camels, crocodiles, bears, wolves, and even elephants were all shipped to Rome to die in the Colosseum for the entertainment of the people.

Index

Africa 9, 29, 34, 35
Alps, the 29
amphitheater 24
amphorae (jars) 36, 45
Anatolia (Turkey) 31
ancestors 31
animals 8, 12, 19, 20, 21, 22, 24, 25, 26, 27, 29, 30, 31, 34, 35, 45
apartment blocks 40, 41
Apodyterium 17
Appian Way 23
Aquae Sulis (Bath) 17
aqueducts 12, 23
arches 23, 24
architecture 17, 22, 23, 27, 31, 40
armor 28
– helmets 9, 25, 28, 44
army 11, 23, 28, 29, 38, 43
– legions 28
– soldiers 28
– troops 23, 24, 28
art 9, 22, 45
– sculpture 9, 33, 42, 45
– wall paintings 18, 31, 38
assembly 11

bakeries/ baking 13, 37
banks/bankers 44
baths, 14, 16, 17, 23, 28
blacksmiths 26, 38, 39
boats 42
brewing 35
bridges 11, 22, 23
– Milvian 23
Britain 17, 28, 29, 35, 43
building 10, 22, 23 24, 27, 31, 39, 40
business 10, 12, 18, 42, 45

Caere (Etruscan city) 9
Caesar, Julius 30, 45
canals 42
carpenters 26
Carthage (North Africa) 29
carvings 31, 38, 39
ceremonies 30
Cerveteri, Italy 9
chariot races 20, 26, 27
charms 20
children 16, 19, 20, 21, 33
China 45
Cicero (statesman) 20, 34, 40
Circus Maximus 11, 26, 27
cities 10, 37, 38, 40
citizens 11, 18, 34
city-states 8
class
– lower 18
– upper 11, 18, 19, 30, 36
cloth 12, 20, 38, 44
– dye 38, 45
clothing 18, 20, 30, 38, 45
coins 11, 24, 39, 43, 44
colonies 9
Colosseum 11, 24, 45
concrete 22
conquests 39
consuls 11
cooking 36, 37
cosmetics 19
countryside 15, 34, 41, 44

crafts 8, 9, 12, 18, 38, 39
cults 30, 31

dancing 31
death 19, 24, 25, 31
defense 28
democracy 11
disease 29
drama 27
– comedies 27
drink 14, 35

East, the 9, 35
education 19, 21
Egypt 20, 21, 31
elections 11
emperors 8, 10, 11, 19, 22, 24, 26, 28, 30, 31, 36
– Augustus 10, 11, 30
– Caracalla 16
– Claudius 42
– Commodus 30
– Constantine 31
– Hadrian 22, 28, 32
– Titus 24
– Trajan 42, 45
– Vespasian 24
engineering 22
engines 22
entertainment 14, 15, 24, 45
Etruria (Tuscany) 8, 9, 23
Etruscans 8, 9
Europe 9, 10, 22, 35
executions 25
exercise 16, 17
exporting 44

fabrics 18, 38
– silk 45
families 11, 12, 18, 19, 20, 21, 33, 34, 41
farming 8, 34, 35, 38
– crops 8, 34
fashion 18, 19
fighting 10, 25, 28, 29
fires 11, 40, 41
Flavian Amphitheater (see: Colosseum)
food 12, 13, 14, 15, 34, 35, 36, 37, 38, 44, 45
– bread 12, 13, 36, 37
– cereals 23, 34, 35
– fish 12, 19, 36, 37, 45
– flour 13, 23
– fruit 12, 34, 36, 43
– garum 37
– herbs 12, 37
– honey 35
– meals 36, 37
– meat 12, 32, 35, 36, 37
– olives 34, 36, 37
– spices 12, 37
– vegetables 12, 36, 37
fortifications 29
forts 28
Forum, 10, 12, 30
fountains 23, 33
freedom 18, 19, 25
furnaces 17, 38
furnishings 32, 33, 40

gambling 14
games 16, 20, 24, 25, 45

gardens 33
generals 24, 28, 29
Germany 33, 45
gladiators 10, 18, 24, 25
glass 18, 37, 38, 39, 40, 41, 45
gods and goddesses 9, 11, 30, 31
– Bacchus 31
– Cybele 31
– Dionysus 31
– Fortuna 31
– household 31
– Isis 31
– Janus 11
– Juno 30
– Jupiter 11, 30
– Mercury 44
– Mithras 31
– Neptune 43
– tribal 9
– Vesta 30
– Zeus 30
gold 12, 18, 19, 20, 28, 39, 44
government 11, 13
grain 13, 23, 43
graves 8, 18
Greece 9, 21, 22, 23, 27, 29, 30, 31, 35

hairstyles 18, 20
Hannibal (general) 29
harbor 42
hardware 12
harvesting 34
heating 17, 41
Hercules 30
heroes 9, 30, 31
homes 15, 18, 21, 31, 39
hospitals 28
hotels 14, 15
households 19, 21, 32, 33
houses 9, 12, 14, 18, 23, 28, 32, 33, 37, 38, 40

importing 35, 44, 45
India 18, 45
industry 38, 44
ink 21
inns 14
inventions 22, 28
Iran 31
Iron Age 8, 9
Italy 8, 9, 28, 29, 34, 35, 41
ivory 18, 39

jewelry 9, 18, 19, 38, 39
justice 11

kitchens 12, 14, 15, 36, 37, 40

laborers 34
landowners 11, 34, 44
language 9, 21
– Latin 21
lavatories 23, 40
law 11, 14
lead 19, 23
leather 20, 35
literature 21
luxuries 45

machines 22, 28
magistrates 11
manufacturing 38
markets 12, 14, 43
– Trajan's 12
marriage 19, 20
masks 27
mass production 38, 44
Medieval period 9
Mediterranean
– region 44
– Sea 37, 43
merchants 42, 43, 44, 45
metals 8, 9, 18, 21, 28, 36, 37, 39, 41, 43, 44
– bronze 9, 21, 31, 36, 44
– silver 28, 32, 34, 39, 44, 45
Milan, Edict of 31
mills 13, 23
mining 22, 39
money 15, 18, 44
mosaics 13, 16, 25, 32, 38
music 31
mystery cults 31
myths 9, 30

officials 10, 11, 14
oil 12, 16, 19, 34, 39, 41
Ostia, Port of 14, 42

palaces 8, 11, 16, 36
Palatine Hill 8
Pantheon, the 22
paper 21
papyrus 21
patricians 11
patrons 26
Paul (Christian Apostle) 11
perfumes 45
pirates 45
plebians 11
plumbing 23
politics 10, 11, 24, 28, 30
Pompeii 45
poverty 11, 12, 18, 20, 36, 44, 45
port 42, 43, 45
– Portus Romae 42
pottery 23, 35, 36, 39, 45
– Samian ware 39
Praetorian Guard 28
priests and priestesses 30, 31
prisons 28
property 18, 19, 41
provinces 34, 35
public speaking 11, 21

reading 21
religion 10, 30, 31
– Christianity 19, 31
– Mithraism 31
– offerings 30
– rites 31
– sacrifices 19, 30
– worship 30, 31
restaurants 14
rivers 23
– Rhine River 43
– Rhone River 43
– Tiber River 11, 42, 44
roads 22, 23, 35

Roman Empire 10, 11, 14, 19, 22, 23, 28, 30, 33, 35
Roman Republic 8, 10, 11, 29, 42, 44
Romulus and Remus 9

Sardinia, Italy 9
Senate, the 11, 30
Seneca (playwright) 27
sewers 22, 23
ships 42, 43, 44, 45
shops 10, 12, 13, 32, 40
shrines 31
Sicily, Italy 8
silk 18, 38, 45
slaves 12, 15, 19, 20, 21, 22, 25, 26, 27, 32, 34, 36, 39, 43
social life 16, 18, 19
soldiers 28, 29, 31
Spain 29, 35, 39
spinning 38
spirits 20, 31
– lares 31
– penates 31
stables 28
stadium 24
statues 31, 39
stone 23, 27, 28, 38, 42
stoves 14, 37, 41
streets 12, 13, 23, 38

taverns 14, 15
teachers 21
technology 22, 23
temples 22, 31
theater 27
tools 22, 39
towns 10, 34
toys 20
trade 10, 12, 14, 18, 23, 38, 43, 44, 45
transportation 35, 38, 44
travel 14, 15, 23
Turkey 31
Tuscany, Italy 8

vehicles 35
Vestal Virgins 30
Vesuvius, Mount 35
villages 8, 10
villas 32, 36

walls 11, 17, 28, 41
war 10
– Punic Wars 29
– siege 28, 29
water 2, 12, 14, 23, 37, 40, 44
wealth 8, 10, 11, 12, 18, 20, 21, 34, 36, 39, 40, 44, 45
weapons 9, 25, 28, 29, 39
weaving 38
windows 40, 41
wine 12, 14, 30, 31, 35, 36, 37, 45
– vineyards 35
women 14, 16, 18, 19, 25, 30, 31, 38, 43
wood 20, 27, 35, 37, 41, 43
wool 18, 35
writing 21